Rebecca Hood

Astrology

For beginners

A Complete Guide to Discover the Secrets of Astrology

Table of Contents

The Truth About Astrology

It is said that astrology is the order that shows us how to make horoscopes and utilize the places of heavenly bodies, to comprehend and decipher human presence on Earth, at any rate, what it says on the main astrology site. I regularly experience articles and remarks that keep thinking about whether astrology is a science or attempting to demonstrate or discredit astrology in logical terms. I don't perceive how similarity can be drawn between astrology and present-day science. Science and astrology are two altogether different controls, in view of totally different standards. Science follows the standards of experimentation, perception and induction; the logical standards must have hypothetical or numerical proof that must consistently be reliable. In spite of the fact that astrology has its own arrangement of all around characterized standards, they are altogether different from those of science.

Regardless of what numerous crystal gazers may guarantee, astrology isn't unbounded, and before we can announce Astrology, one science or another, we should comprehend what these are. It is accepted that astrology (Vedic) is the result of perfect motivation and was sent to the Hindu sage, 'Bhrigu' by the goddess of abundance, 'Mahalakshmi.' This information was recorded in antiquated consecrated writings, of which just remaining parts. Astrology is certifiably not an ideal order and is comparable to the soothsayer who rehearses it. Their fitness decides the precision of the outcomes. Generally, it relies upon their profundity of information, the sort of involvement (nature of the forecasts made) and the term of the experience. In any case, it is sensible to accept that even a celestial prophet, who in all regards is all around acknowledged, can't profess to have total information on astrology since his insight can't go past the substance of the writings that actually exist, in light of the fact that the last themselves are inadequate.

As clarified on an astrology site, science and astrology depend on oppositely contradicted sees, as science consistently manages energizing inquiries regarding the universe, the production of the universe, the chance of equal universes, which limits a small amount of a second after the Big Bang and the get-go.

All in all, what was there before the get-go? On the off chance that the universe has kept growing since its creation, what does it reach out into? Our insight is restricted to such an extent that these inquiries appear to be silly. Vedic astrology, then again, comes from a conviction framework that depends on the rule that clarification for all that exists can be found in The Hindu sacred writings or with their assistance. Numerous Vedic researchers accept that what researchers find today was known to the sages constantly. For instance, the twin Vedic planets, 'Rahu' and 'Ketu' are one of a kind to Vedic astrology. They are said to speak to a legendary snake, with 'Rahu' as the head and 'Ketu' as the tail. These two planets are viewed as malevolent and eat up different types of energy, for example, endless wells and obscure or debilitate the sun and Moon. The shade of 'Rahu' is dark, and of'Ketu' is dim. The closeness among 'Rahu' and 'Ketu' and dark openings is very astonishing; the furthest edge of a dark opening is viewed as a smaller white person. Another case being referred to and recorded on principle astrology site referenced above is the importance of the number "108", which is the number of globules on a rosary of Hindu supplication dabs. Even though these supplication dabs result from the old Vedic period, on account of present-day science, we currently realize that the figure "108" is vital since the separation between the Earth and the sun is around multiple times the measurement of the sun. The width of The Sun is around multiple times that of the Earth, and the separation between the Earth and the Moon is around multiple times the distance across of the

Moon. Is it conceivable that the antiquated Hindu sages could decide these heavenly estimations, with such accuracy, well before the presence of telescopes?

Obviously, nothing from what was just mentioned demonstrates anything logically; however, it contemplates whether science is truly exceptional enough to clarify Astrology. As I would like to think, to clarify or expose astrology, a researcher should initially comprehend and have involvement in astrology standards and must have the option to rehearse astrology. I figure the individual would comprehend that mysterious expectations are not parallel in nature, not all things are highly contrasting, as in science, and there are credible shades of dim.

Notwithstanding being utilized to make forecasts about the future, Vedic astrology likewise takes into account remedial measures, using valuable stones, charms, petition services, serenades of mantras, and so forth

As indicated by the old Vedic sacred writings, an equal universe, complete with planets, stars, heavenly bodies, and so forth, exists in the human body. Clearly, this universe doesn't exist in a similar actual structure as we probably are aware ofspace science. Notwithstanding, its reality can be experienced by the enlivening of the "kundalini" or "dozing snake" a splendid string going through the spinal line, the enlivening of which is the most elevated stage in "tantric" rehearses. Vedic astrology perceives nine planets, twelve zodiacs and 28-star groupings. Pandit Sarvesh Nagarvedic, the main stargazer at the astrology site referenced above, clarifies that the nine Vedic planets have gotten mythical being status; notwithstanding, these heavenly bodies are not almighty and depend on contributions made on Earth for quality. When on Earth, we supplicate or apace the force that speaks to a planet, gaining its valuable stone or Yantra, we really resort to the intensity of the planet, present in our equal universe. Along these lines, the planets are handily fulfilled and react by giving their gifts to their admirers.

All in all, what does this mean? Are there in paradise or in us the very powers that control our carries on with under Astrology? "As it is higher up, it is likewise inside," is by all accounts the appropriate response. Celestial impacts are not inaccessible articles that work in segregation; they are essential for the universe of which we are likewise part, and we have the way to reinforce or pacify them, as we wish. This doesn't imply that we can totally change destiny; it would mean being able to change the situation of the planets in our horoscopes, which is clearly outlandish. What we have to recall is that regardless of Astrology, everybody is experiencing acceptable and awful occasions. The essential rule of astrology is that activities and (Karam) are over the alert, much the same as God, astrology enables the individuals who to support themselves, yet utilizing our insight into astrology, we can change the impacts of the powers of the zodiac, so you can take advantage of the great occasions and capitalize on them.

Types of Astrology

Astrology is the investigation of the connection between the overall places of some divine bodies and life here on Earth. Since the word astrology comes from the Greek words Astron, signifying 'star' and logos, signifying "word", we can in a real sense interpret astrology to mean the language of the stars; a language and practice that have created more than a huge number of years by numerous societies around the globe from its initial starting, recorded in the third thousand years before the century's end.

Indian or Jyotish, the establishment of Jyotisha depends on the Sanskrit Bandhu of the Vedas, which portrays the relationship between the inward and external universes. Similarly, as with Western astrology, Jyotisha depends on the association between the microcosm and the world. The microcosm is life on Earth, while the cosmos is the universe.

The historical backdrop of astrology

In spite of the fact that the terms astrology and space science have for quite some time been inseparable from one another, Astrology really goes before stargazing and brain research. The most seasoned realized celestial declarations go back to Babylon in the far off 1645 BC. Notwithstanding, the historical backdrop of astrology doesn't follow a specific course of events, yet three autonomous branches that we call Western astrology, Indian or Jyotish astrology and Chinese or Eastern Asian astrology.

Chinese

Like Western and Indian astrology, it is accepted that Chinese astrology started in China in the third thousand years. Like the airtight law," as above, as beneath, "says Confucius," paradise sends its fortunate or unfortunate images, and shrewd acts in consequential astrology in China was then joined with Chinese practice known as Feng shui.

Western

It was accepted that the investigation of Western astrology was first drilled among the old Babylonians in the third thousand years BC. The Babylonians accepted that the divine beings were liable for all environmental marvels, for example, downpour and sun. Egypt additionally has a significant spot in celestial history. Star graphs going back to 4,200 BC show that Egypt has an old history with astrology. Pyramids are likewise arranged toward the North Pole of the sky, as they filled in as mysterious mini-computers, just as entombment places for celestial Pharaohs. Truth be told, Ramses II is regularly credited with fixing the places of the cardinal signs Aries, Cancer, Libra and Capricorn. Some zodiac signs are likewise supposed to be of Egyptian root, including Aries and Leo.

Houses and indications of the zodiac that remain basically unaltered today.

As Europeans turned out to be more educated, a few periodicals and chronicles started to distribute prophetic data. Among the exceptional creators are Galileo and Copernicus, who rehearsed crystal gazers and organizers of the cutting edge logical development. Notwithstanding, the more famous astrology turned into, the more it was analyzed. Furthermore, when the fundamental celestial expectations didn't work out, Astrology started to fall into decay.

It was just a lot later, with the introduction of Princess Margaret in 1930, that astrology encountered a recovery. To celebrate her introduction to the world, the British paper, London Sunday Express, distributed the princess's visionary profile, consequently offering life to the paper's cutting edge horoscope section.

Horoscope

Created in Hellenistic Egypt, horoscopic astrology utilizes a visual portrayal of the sky called horoscope, gotten from the Greek word, horoscopes, which signifies "a gander at the hours."This visual portrayal ordinarily appears as a table or a chart (beneath), which speaks to the places of the sun, moon, planets, the prophetic perspectives, and points at the hour of a specific occasion, similar to the introduction of an individual.

Horoscope astrology is partitioned into four fundamental parts of Christmas, common, elective and hourly.

1. Christmas astrology is the most normally rehearsed type of horoscope astrology and depends on the possibility that the character or way of every person in life can be controlled by building a natal graph for the specific date, time and spot of the birth of an individual.

2. Common astrology is probably the most seasoned type of astrology and is named after the Roman word Mundus, which signifies "the world."Common astrology depends on the possibility that there is a connection among people and world occasions, world issues (wars, murders, and so forth), and land wonders, for example, seismic tremors.

3. Political decision astrology is the act of deciding a person's visionary profile to decide how and when to take an interest in a specific business or occasion, for example, starting a business.

4. Hourly astrology is the training wherein the stargazer endeavors to respond to a person's particular inquiry by building a horoscope fixated on that particular inquiry. For instance, "will I get an advancement at work?"

The Meaning Behind Astrology Symbols

The images of astrology are not the disclosure of the century. Individuals have known the images of astrology for a long time. For a long time, mysterious images have been utilized to speak to various zodiac signs. Whenever you have taken in the importance behind the images of astrology, you understand that they are anything but difficult to recall and perceive. The images of astrology speak to certain indications of the zodiac, so the zodiac indications can be recognized from one another.

Aquarius is viewed as the most recognizable image of astrology. This image of astrology is constantly given figures, which look like water. Somebody can interface the waves in the picture of the indication of astrology with an aquarium, however, not with water. Notwithstanding, the astrology sign Aquarius is presumably the most effortless to recall.

Other celestial signs simple to recall are Taurus and Aries. The picture of the prophetic sign Taurus speaks to a Taurus. Its name can be handily recollected in light of the fact that the Spanish word for Taurus is the equivalent. A circle with two Taurus horns is generally the picture of the indication of astrology Taurus. Then again, the astrology sign Aries is related with a goat, and its picture shows the horns on the top of a goat.

In the zodiac, there are two celestial images. That is the reason fish and twins frequently blend. Once in a while, their pictures are very comparable. The figure of the prophetic sign Pisces is generally given two Pisces. The picture of the astrology indication of Pisces is consistently a couple of Pisces. The indication of astrology Gemini, then again, is given a picture suggestive of the Roman Number II.

One of the most unmistakably perceived visual pictures of astrology images is what speaks to the indication of astrology Leo. The mane of a lion or just a lion is the image of the astrology of the lion.

Virgo and Scorpio are additionally very comparable prophetic images. These two images of astrology take after the letter M. these strikingly various images of astrology are spoken to by very comparative symbols. The distinction between the pictures is that the image of astrology Scorpio has a "tail" that holds fast to the tip of a bolt outward. The "tail" of the Virgin is internal and has no bolt at its end.

Disease and Sagittarius are two images of astrology, which are anything but difficult to recognize. While the indication of malignancy is very ladylike, the indication of Sagittarius is manly. The astrology malignant growth image comprises of two meeting circles. The image of Sagittarius astrology is spoken to simply by a bolt facing up and to one side.

Capricorn is likely the weirdest image of astrology. I don't have a clue why; however, their prophetic image speaks to a goatfish. A goatfish isn't the most wonderful picture conceivable; however, I think the image isn't so awful. The last image of astrology, which remains, is Libra. This image of astrology looks like the balance of equity we find in the courts. They are normally connected with balance.

These images of astrology live for some ages and will most likely anticipate that a lot more should come.

Astrology and Mankind

American Heritage Dictionary characterizes astrology as the investigation of the positions and parts of heavenly bodies in the conviction that they have an effect on the course of common natural occasions and human issues. Planetary perception is the premise of astrology. The act of astrology was boundless even on old occasions.

The historical backdrop of astrology is a significant piece of progress and returns to the beginning of mankind. A portion of the world's realized human advancements has broadly utilized this field. For instance, the old Chinese development, the Egyptian human progress, the antiquated Indian human progress, and so forth, all astrology rehearsed at some time. Middle Easterners additionally rehearsed astrology before the approach of Islam. The Arabs were the very best in class in the field of Astronomy.

The antiquated Babylonians were most likely the first to utilize astrology. The Babylonians were the first to name the times of the week after the sun, moon, and planets. They were additionally the first to characterize the twelve places of the zodiac. Baghdad and Damascus were known as focuses of astrology and Astronomy on antiquated occasions. Egypt contributed extraordinarily to the advancement of astrology. It is accepted that a portion of the mysterious indications of the zodiac began in Egypt.

The Greek cosmologist Ptolemy was the main individual to compose a book on astrology. He systematized the astrology of the Sun sign we know today. Ptolemy attempted to anticipate the places of divine bodies among themselves and the Earth by knowing their orbital developments. During the right time, astrology was essential for space science. Afterward, cosmology turned into a definite science, and astrology remained part of religious philosophy.

Chinese astrology demands the five components, metal, wood, water, fire and Earth. The zodiac signs utilized by them are additionally unique in relation to different types of astrology.

India has a rich history of astrology. Astrology was polished even on Vedic occasions in India. Astrology is one of the six orders of Vedanga. Indeed, even the old Hindu sacred writings join incredible significance to the different parts of planetary developments and their consequences for people. Astrology is as yet examined and rehearsed by numerous individuals in India.

It is viewed as crucial in Indian culture. It is utilized to settle on choices about marriage, start new organizations and move to another home, and so forth. Hindus accept that human karma or misery in life is because of karma, and karma must be impacted by the developments of the planets. Among Hindus, the Brahmins are viewed as the best experts in astrology.

Celestial prophets in India contend that this is a logical technique for anticipating what's to come. They actually have clubs in this field of study in the boundaries of Hinduism. Hindus consistently put stock in mysterious forecasts. Truth be told, strict Hindus can't envision existence without Astrology. An ever-increasing number of Indians started to assemble their homes as indicated by the standards of Vastu Shashtra.

Celestial ramifications additionally administer this old Indian convention. Hindus accept that the tenants' overall thriving and advantages rely upon Vastu's standards when fabricating the House. Indian celestial prophets guarantee that they can demonstrate that mysterious forecasts are truly logical.

Horoscope is a piece of astrology. Every day horoscope perusing has become a pattern even in the created nations of the West. The Western psyche has consistently put any subject under investigation and will, in general, depend exclusively on logical realities.

Yet, this doesn't keep Westerners from fixating on their horoscopes. Out of nowhere, the Western world understood the chance of knowing and improving their future with astrology utilization. An ever-increasing number of Westerners started to have faith in the chance of being hit by ground-breaking planets and stars.

Western specialists have remembered the subject of astrology for their examination. Astrology has never been analyzed and concentrated as it has as of late. In such a manner, Indian soothsayers must introduce themselves and show the world the intensity of astrology.

Cornerstones of Astrology - Planets, Signs, Houses and Aspects

Perusing the diagrams is the oblivious objective of all who study astrology, regardless of whether they don't understand it. You can take any apprentice book or mysterious Journal and read what others have expounded on the various pieces of astrology. What he needs to accomplish most actually is the capacity to look in the driver's seat and unravel what he says and what it implies. This requires individual exertion, great memory and time.

Astrology Sun sign is extremely mainstream and is viewed as day by day, week after week or month to month small readings made for the twelve signs. I composed a ton of a section for magazines and papers, just as radio and TV programs. A genuine exertion is expected to change these straightforward sentences, particularly those with which you recognize intently. You can't simply take sentences behind closed doors,or you shouldn't, on the grounds that a few audience members, in a real sense, take what you state. I regularly thought somebody followed me, to be exact. On different occasions, it resembles the section communicates in an unknown dialect that has nothing to do with me. Exactness has to do with the stargazer's ability and the receptivity of the crowd.

Astrology Sun sign is nonexclusive in nature. What might be compared to a petition routed to 1/12 of the total populace needs to associate with somebody, isn't that right? A great many people realize their Sun sign to know which supplication to peruse. If you know your rising sign, you can get double the mileage of the segment, and you will somehow recognize yourself with these expressions. Add your moon sign, and you can get a little more modest pieces from this segment. I question that even elegantly composed and precise sun oriented board sections can give considerably more to the man on the road who has a shallow comprehension of sunlight based boards. Astrology Sun sign is extremely nonexclusive, however exceptionally famous and effectively available, yet it is an abbreviated adaptation of genuine astrology.

Anyway, what is valid about astrology? It is a guide of the sky worked for an individual utilizing the date, time and spot of birth (longitude and scope on the planet). Since two births can't consume the very space while, second make a guide for a person. (We pushed this specific envelope with numerous births, isn't that right? Notwithstanding, my sibling is hitched to a twin, and the Twins are altogether different.) This guide of the moving sky furnishes the celestial prophet with a graph of potential outcomes and aims for this person that can be seen and perused as a moving dynamic. Perusing the diagram is the explanation you go to a celestial prophet and is likewise the way you could get contaminated with the mistake of astrology, so you can do this perusing without help from anyone else. Having existed for a long time and having examined numerous self-improvement strategies, astrology is, without a doubt, the best strategy I have found to get myself and my life. When you get an example of what you can accomplish for you, you need more, regardless of whether you need to attempt to get more.

At the point when you take a gander at a guide of the sky that is yours, a guide pretty much you and your life, the sky is actually the cutoff. A wide range of new entryways additionally opens the principle entry way of the Sun sign that you can peruse in your neighborhood paper. There are different bodies other than the sun, which are all things considered called planets. I know, I know. The sun isn't a planet; it is a star. The moon isn't a planet; it is a satellite of the Earth. It is simpler to tell the planets altogether than The Sun, Moon and planets. Rehash after me "simplicity of reference, simplicity of reference."

In this way, we have the 12 Sun Signs (You have to learn them all, not simply your Sun sign) and planets, which incredibly extended what we at first expected to consider. If you take a gander in the driver's seat given when you dispatch your Sky Map, you will see 12 wheel portions like the orange or grapefruit sections contained with the natural product expand. The wheel speaks to the wheel of life. It's the land we're all on, earth to earth, actual reality, all that. Since the entirety of this without a moment's delay is hard to comprehend, we advantageously partition it into more modest portions called houses. The entire wheel speaks to the individual's entire existence, and the 12 divisions speak to portions of that life, or what I call sands of interest. There is a section for your actual body and yourself. There's a portion for your folks and family. There is a portion for your calling and vocation, etc. Every division covers around 1/12 of its size, so it is exceptionally small; the compartments are brimming with issues. Add this to what you have to comprehend to make a perusing. We currently have three classifications, with a ton of work. However, it is a significant classification.

Perspectives are the most exceptional region of astrology learning. Why would that be? The angles ought to expect that you definitely know the planets, the signs and the houses since you need to cause them to associate or shape connections. Angles are not, at this point, troublesome as a theme, yet you need the other three classes of work before you can bode well and the ability to apply perspectives in a perusing.

If I were proposing an examination management, I would recommend sunlight-based signs as a decent spot to begin perusing since we have a bit of leeway with the prevalence of astrology Sun sign. Simply realize that this is just a flimsy first layer. Here you will start to become familiar with the idea of signs, an essential for the utilization of planets in these signs. There are 12 signs, yet there are numerous mixes to learn in these signs, for example, cardinal, fixed and impermanent, fire, earth, air and water, images or glyphs, fantasies, and so on

The ten bodies we on the whole call the planets would be my next recommendation to consider on the grounds that the planets will turn out to be increasingly more significant as they build up their mysterious capacity. Study them each in turn and top to bottom, on the grounds that each speaks to a core value, impact or energy comparable to life.

At that point, he contemplates celestial houses in the entirety of their wonder. Each house speaks to 1/12 of your background, so every little house is brimming with issues and occasions. There's actually a long way to go, so take as much time as is needed. You have your life to follow this examination.

To wrap things up, to examine the angles. As referenced, the mix spoke to by the rakish connection between two bodies or focuses expects you to comprehend the two bodies or focuses exclusively before examining the relationship shaped between them. Perspectives can get into your face and require your consideration. Signs and houses will likewise enter this demonstration, so study the angles whenever you have taken in the language of the other three classes. This is your essential examination management, the request wherein to contemplate the four classifications.

Presently I need to change the speed regarding the request of significance in the application or perusing. My best similarity for an amateur understudy is to consider building a house. Above all else, the nation, city, area, region, part, structural plans and the developer, all the vital fundamental works are chosen. Mysteriously picks the sort of astrology, Eastern or Western (sidereal or tropical), geocentric or heliocentric, realistic and wheel type, characterizes its objective: all starter stages prompting the setup of the guide of the sky itself. This carries us to what could be compared to establishing the framework of the House. At this stage, the wheel may appear as though a spaghetti dish should be fixed and decoded.

Normally, in the wake of putting the base, the foundations are set. In our similarity, the structure presently has a guide or measurement to the normal progression of what is to come. Celestial foundations are planets, signs, houses and viewpoints. When your wheel is arranged and noticeable, you will proceed onward to the four classes referenced above to comprehend this guide of the sky and utilize the data created by your investigation of the four classifications to peruse or decipher it. However long you have an arrangement and work on the arrangement, you will be astonished at how much data you can get from this sky map. This brilliant arrangement of data will continually increment as you build up your insight and aptitudes through experience. On the first occasion, when I composed a table read, I created over twelve pages of data about an all-out outsider. He was confused; the outsider was astounded. He had additionally clung. It was 36 years back I actually do Astrology.

We have four foundations that ought to have concentrated steadily and, gratitude to this examination, built up a bunch of data about each. One of these foundations must turn into the foundation, which drives or controls data progression for this diagram. The request I offered them to concentrate presently should change as the normal key classification advances. The foundation is the planets. Planets "control" signs and houses, and you will find perspectives (precise connections) that may appear to be fundamentally the same as the idea of certain planets.

The vast majority of what we can realize and apply can be characterized as what, where, when, why and how of presence. We can figure out what, where, why and how through these four birth classes.

- What about our lives, as standards, energies, driving forces and inspirations, are planets

- The spot of our carries on with, for example, points, occasions, fields of interest are the houses

- How our carries on with, for example, mentalities, articulations, motions or shading, are the signs.

- Why our carries on with, for example, stress, struggle, karma, stream, or tightening are the perspectives

- When is a local and dynamic individual realistic capacity

It's simple. When you become familiar with the essential standards of the four classes, the rest is application and experience. Your expertise grows normally and consecutively. There is in every case more to examine, yet the improvement of a coordinated assemblage of data that you have set aside the effort to solidify in your cognizance is the thing that gives the premise to all that you can and will do. In the event that you hold back on examining these classes, you'll have a frail, permeable base, openings in your insight that can stagger each time until you occupy those vacant spaces in your celestial aptitude toolbox. I know since I've been there and I've done this. These four classifications are the spot for you to begin constructing a strong establishment of prophetic information that will discover no limit to apply to your life. On the off chance that I lament anything about my mysterious examinations, it is that I have not begun previously. Beforehand, I would have made my life more reasonable, particularly during the most troublesome scenes.

Make the most of your dinner. A heterogeneous virtual celestial blend anticipates you restricted simply by the cutoff points you put or permit them to be set there. The universe (and its Creator) gave us a monster guide of potential and plausibility and gave us enough minds to build up the capacity to understand it. Go to him!

Astrology: A Science or Superstition?

People have consistently been interested in their future. At whatever point somebody is in a difficult situation and can not effectively receive in return, he needs to know whether the times of his hopelessness will end. What's more, provided that this is true, when? At the point when a great deal of time, exertion or cash is put resources into a venture, it is normal to contemplate whether this speculation will pay off. There have consistently been individuals who have effectively anticipated future occasions. Their techniques were extraordinary: a few people can plan ahead, some utilized Tarot cards, some draw up a prophetic card that we call horoscopes, some read lines on individuals' palms. It can't be rejected that the future has been precisely anticipated ordinarily and by numerous individuals. Each effective forecast shows that it is truly conceivable to foresee the future accurately.

In old occasions, celestial prophets were profoundly regarded by individuals. There was no distinction between cosmologists and stargazers. Truth be told, space science and astrology were not viewed as two distinct subjects. Many will be amazed to discover that the greater part of the past's prestigious researchers, including Sir Isaac Newton, were likewise stargazers. In antiquated India, astrology was known as "Jyotish Shastra" which included prescient astrology and what we know as cosmology. Obviously, the celestial prophets of that time were additionally extraordinary mathematicians. A quintessential stargazer was classified as "Trikal-darshee": the person who could see the past, the present and what's to come. Maybe it would not be a misrepresentation to state that astrology was viewed as the main part of science.

Gradually, throughout some stretch of time, this issue has fallen into notoriety.

How does astrology lose its magnified status?

It is an unavoidable truth that individuals impersonate effective, well known and regarded individuals. Seeing the economic wellbeing appreciated by soothsayers, The Charlatans started to mask themselves as celestial prophets. They took in certain little-known techniques and started to trick simple individuals. It was and stayed an entirely beneficial business. A soothsayer brings in lucrative forecasts, with no assurance that any of his expectations will end up being valid. When a stargazer makes a shop, individuals start to go to him with the expectation that he can accurately anticipate his future. The celestial prophet is in a magnificent position. For instance, you can make expectations on ten individuals, getting just one right forecast. The nine individuals, whom he erroneously anticipated, will stay away for the indefinite future to him. In any case, the 10th individual, whose crystal gazer could effectively anticipate, won't just re-visitation of him, yet will likewise re-visitation of numerous others, referring to individual experience. Along these lines, the movement of a soothsayer consistently thrives, regardless of the amount he, when all is said and done, enters his calling. However, the disservice of this was that crystal gazers, as a gathering, started to think about numerous questionable individuals as legislators of the cutting edge time. When such an impression started to make strides, astrology as a subject was not, at this point, alluring to wise individuals. Individuals who had the ability started to seek different subject matters. Throughout some stretch of time, the inescapable occurred. No ability, deserving at least some respect, decided to seek after astrology as a job or a side interest and the consequence of this is for the general public's viewing pleasure it in the current occasions.

There was another significant motivation behind why astrology got one of the minor subject matters. It was the decay of India, the wellspring of human development, and its loss of the status of the depositary of all information on the old world (perceive how India lost its brilliance). The Islamic crowds, who assaulted and looted India a few times and afterward decided that nation for a very long time, had no regard for invaluable masterpieces, heavenly engineering and other lifted up zones of human exertion. They pulverized the vast majority of the antiquated sanctuaries, consumed libraries like Nalanda and Takshshila, and unquestionably carried innumerable books of limitless shrewdness to people in the future of humankind. A great deal of recorded information, including mysterious books, was lost. This misfortune was unsalvageable, as Indian culture around then was focused on guaranteeing its endurance and a steady battle against the aggressors. The couple of individuals, who had with them priceless writings and sacred texts, were hard to save the leftover works of the old sages. That is the reason when contemplating astrology; it appears to be that some essential connections are absent. With the

Hindu way of thinking losing its ground, it was normal that astrology would lose its noticeable spot too. As present-day science was created and the logical disposition progressed, with the deficiency of genuine celestial prophets, Astrology started to blur into obscurity.

Analysis and promotion

Individuals deride astrology for two fundamental reasons. To begin with, obviously, is that expectations made by celestial prophets frequently turn out badly. Second, in the event that one carries his horoscope to various stargazers, they make various expectations. They likewise make various horoscopes given a similar arrangement of information identifying with an individual's introduction to the world. These realities power individuals to reason that astrology isn't a science and is only an approach to cool individuals to serve stargazers.

It can't be rejected that the above reasons are legitimate. Nonetheless, there is a component of bias against astrology that also assumes a part in this science's denigration. Let us give a guide to delineate this point.

A man becomes ill due to sickness. He will see his nearby specialist. Your PCP encourages you to step through exams. Subsequent to seeing the consequences of these tests and considering the patient's side effects, the specialist reasons that the man has gotten a specific infection, for instance, the sickness. He recommends certain drugs, and the patient gets back, wanting to dispose of the infection as quickly as time permits. Subsequent to taking the drugs for the following two days, the patient finds that the prescriptions don't function as they should. He returns to the specialist, and the specialist changes the drugs, and the individual quickly starts to react to the second arrangement of prescriptions. Within a couple of days, the individual got back to his old solid self.

What might have occurred if the individual had not reacted to this second arrangement of prescriptions? Doubtlessly he would have gone to another specialist. This specialist would have encouraged him to step through different exams, analyzed his concern dependent on his insight and experience and treated him likewise. Once more, there would have been the very likelihood that the patient would dispose of his disease.

Thus, eventually, it comes down to the issue of the right conclusion. When the sickness is accurately distinguished, it tends to be effectively treated. The specialist's concern is to accurately distinguish the infection, considering the indications and the aftereffects of the tests performed. Truth be told, he surmises the infection as per the patient's manifestations and to validate his intuitions, the specialist requests the patient to go through a specific arrangement from tests. On the off chance that the specialist's first theory is erroneous, he proposes to the patient another arrangement of tests pointed toward affirming his second-best speculation of the illness.

There is another component that can demolish the patient's odds of improving: the test outcomes. In the event that the lab that plays out these tests commits an error, the specialist will undoubtedly be hoodwinked by the outcomes. It has also been consistently seen that even with similar manifestations and similar test outcomes arrangement, various specialists can analyze the issue in an unexpected way.

When it occurs with regards to astrology, something very similar is offered as proof that this isn't a science. At the point when a specialist commits an error, his aptitudes are not credited to clinical science. Yet, on the off chance that a stargazer comes up short, astrology is viewed as pseudo-science. In the event that specialists can arrive at various resolutions dependent on similar information, for what reason should celestial prophets not be permitted to vary from one another? You will more likely than not discover contrasts in your outcomes on the off chance that you take blood tests from similar patients in various research centers. In the event that machines worked with all our logical information available to us commit errors, nobody slanders present-day science. Yet, with regards to astrology, individuals are too ready even to consider rejecting it. Maybe, by doing this, individuals need to demonstrate that they have a supposed logical demeanor.

For what reason are soothsayers mixed up in their forecast?

Absence of information - this is maybe the fundamental explanation. Most celestial prophets, having taken in a bit, think that it's hard to oppose the impulse to begin making forecasts. A specific level of their expectations end up being valid, on the grounds that they took shortly of astrology, all things considered. They can not help, however, show their insane information. Another explanation is the compulsion to begin harvesting, at the earliest opportunity, the products of their endeavors to gain proficiency with the theme. When clients begin going to them, they lose energy to keep finding out additional. Also, they have minimal available chances to put forth more attempts for additional findings. They're too bustling, tricking individuals.

Absence of ability: in present-day times, since the quest for this subject isn't viewed as truly decent, virtuoso individuals don't take the investigation of astrology. They like to become researchers, engineers, specialists, literati, craftsmen, and so forth. This doesn't help the improvement of astrology, nor does it help to add information or locate the missing connections in this theme. Presently, there are no genuine exploration ventures identified with this territory. Along these lines, this information base isn't refreshed.

Mistaken information: since the very premise of astrology is arithmetic, information, for example, the season of birth, and so on, you should be explicit. On the off chance that this information is off base, the horoscope, and, in like manner, its understanding will undoubtedly be inadequate. The area of the cusps, the divisions of the houses and the planetary situations at a given time should likewise be precise. The numerous ephemerides vary such a great amount from one another that it appears to be unfathomable. You have to follow the most precise information (for instance, from NASA) for estimations in this time of science. Ordinarily, celestial prophets will generally take the simple street and follow some sort of things prepared to demonstrate, prompting mistakes in their figures. Destiny of the subject: it might happen that the destiny of the individual who needs to pursue his future doesn't support the individual to know his future. This thought may sound insane; however, it isn't. Indeed, even in present-day times, with all the advancements of clinical science, patients keep on die from treatable sicknesses. In the event that an individual is bound to pass on from pneumonia, he will do this, notwithstanding the way that a huge number of individuals around the globe get effective treatment consistently. In the event that destiny can assume a function here, on the grounds that it can not assume a similar part as astrology. The very idea of things to come: current science separates the universe into two sections: known and obscure. He accepts that all that is obscure today will be distributed tomorrow. For some time, all that will be known one day. In any case, edified sages said that a few parts of presence are mysterious. These things don't have a place in the domain of human information. A few parts of things to come have a place with a similar area. Anybody, who will contemplate astrology with a receptive outlook, can not dismiss it as something without merit. It is a simple undertaking for celestial prophets to precisely express certain things about a man, for example, his actual qualities, the sicknesses that are probably going to be distressed, his personality, his overall accomplishment in life as far as the cash he acquires or the popularity he accomplishes, the idea of your calling, and so forth basically by taking a gander at your horoscope is accurately drawn. It is in the subtleties and timing of occasions that crystal gazers will, in general, be mixed up. What is required is another way to deal with the issue. Brilliant personalities need to take it for study, right a few irregularities and misinterpretations that this science has gained before. Subsequently, just this subject can recapture its legitimate spot as a genuine and significant part of information.

Astrology System

Astrology is the blend of convictions, framework and conventions that can give future data about human character, natural issues and human connections. The individual who rehearses this astrology is called a soothsayer. Most soothsayers accept that nature and common things affect the body and human conduct. They accept that nature affects people.

Whenever wanted, frequently, you ought to consider a representative language or fine art or the type of divination. It has endless definitions. Diverse stargazer gave various sorts of definitions, yet every celestial prophet trusts in a single thing that can clarify the present, past and future.

Astrology is considered inaccurate by mainstream researchers. Established researchers called it odd notions, yet the mental network clarifies it emphatically. A few people say that astrology is identified with science.

Astrology has an extraordinary history. Since old occasions, individuals of the world have rehearsed this thing. Before 3000 BC, individuals rehearsed it, which is recorded. It assumes a significant function in the arrangement of World culture. Astrology has a relationship with cosmology, Vedas and different kinds of authentic occurrences. A couple of hundreds of years prior, astrology and stargazing were viewed as the equivalent. After the eighteenth century, when the Renaissance started, Astrology was isolated from space science. Indeed, even now, the celestial prophet depends on cosmology to break down Astrology. A few celestial prophets actually feel that astrology is the piece of cosmology.

The word astrology comes from the Latin expression "Astrology"(Astronomy). It was gotten from the Greek word Astron (star), and "Logia" signifies study. Thus, the investigation of the star is Astrology. From the historical backdrop of astrology, we can undoubtedly comprehend that it is identified with cosmology.

Most celestial things depend on the development of stars and the planet. Planets are endorsed by specific images. Astrology likewise shows the mathematical and rakish connection between various sorts of planets and occasions. From this inquiry, characterize a wide range of human instinct and mishaps.

As indicated by Western convention, prescient Astrology clarifies two techniques, one is prophetic travels, and the other is mysterious movements. The strategy for mysterious travels clarifies the development of the planets. In the visionary movement technique, the horoscope advances, as indicated by the setup strategy.

Before, the soothsayer noticed just divine bodies and their development; however, today, the people groups of the world have gained incredible ground here. In spite of the fact that there is an extraordinary contention about astrology, a few people actually have confidence in it and attempt to adhere to the principles of astrology. At that point, it's up to an individual how he will take this.

Charting the Basics of Astrology

Do you know the fundamentals of astrology? Astrology is one of those old "sciences" that numerous individuals are as yet captivated with; however, they don't know significantly more on which page of the neighborhood paper their horoscope will show up. Anyway, what are the fundamentals of astrology?

In this book, we'll investigate a portion of the things you have to think about astrology. Above all else, how about we take a gander at what it is and where it is suspected to come from. Thus, how about we see what shapes the visionary diagram. At last, we will take a gander at astrology and horoscope.

The essentials of astrology: before all else

It is said that astrology comes to the extent the Babylonians in the second thousand years BC, making it by a wide margin perhaps the most established science". "Astrology" has a similar Latin root (astrology) as "cosmology" despite the fact that the two are currently considered totally extraordinary regarding logical legitimacy. Notwithstanding, in the good 'ol days, it will be considered the other way, with astrology having a solid association with religion.

What makes celestial outline?

A mysterious diagram is a method of following planets and incorporates the sun and the moon. However, it does exclude the Earth since it is the point from which we see different planets.

The image is isolated into twelve "houses" each house speaks to one part of life. The houses are (in Latin and interpretation): Vita (life), Lucrum (abundance), Fratres (siblings), father (parent), Nati (kids), Valetudo (wellbeing), uxor (life partner), Mors (demise), ITER (voyages), Regnum (Kingdom), Benefacta (kinship) and Carcer (jail).

Bird eyes of you may have seen that ten planets and twelve houses leave two void houses, yet dread not, both void houses are viewed as aspects of your life that have been dominated in an alternate life.

The primary thing concentrated on an astrology table is the sun's indication, which is controlled by the sun's situation. The places of the planets are examined, relying upon the impact they have on the Sun sign. The moon sign is the last to be concentrated by how it identifies with different planets on the visionary graph.

The most well-known prophetic diagram (in the principal days) was the subject of birth. The birth subject was utilized to show what the individual's character would resemble. A natal graph might be set up for somebody later in their life, yet it might appear to be not to look like the individual - this is supposed to be because of the way that different occasions will change an individual's character over the long run.

Where does the astrology and horoscope Link come from in this?

In the first place, the twelve indications of the zodiac were identified with the twelve prophetic houses: Aries (Vita), Taurus (Lucrum), Gemini (Fratres), disease (spawner), Lion (Nati), Virgo (Valetudo), Libra (Uxor), Scorpio (Mors), Sagittarius (ITER), Capricorn (Regnum), Aquarius (Benefacta) and Pisces (Carcer).

This combination of astrology and (Horoscope Astrology) would have started in the Mediterranean toward the finish of the second or early I century BC. The horoscope is a visual outline of the sky and is utilized to decipher the significance of the arrangement of planets right now, as expected. What makes it unique in relation to different types of astrology is that it is more mind-boggling and incorporates different factors, such as "the ascendant," which is the eastern skyline level when it ascends out of sight on the curved. Nonetheless, this goes past the meaning of "rudiments of astrology."

That is, a horoscope is over a great many minutes, the variant of the Natal stargazer and permits the current places of divine bodies, while the Natal celestial prophet is steered into the situations at the hour of birth.

Here we have the essentials of astrology. Obviously, we might have had much more profundity all in all subjects and began to cover translations, and so forth, yet you have to know where you are to comprehend where you are going.

We have seen that astrology, which is the first in the horoscope, we have discovered that astrology depends mostly on somebody's introduction to the world(or something else), and is utilized to show how you will create later on; nonetheless, a Christmas present by an older individual, may not compare to the individual, on account of the other, and afterward, at long last, we have seen that the horoscope is basically an approach to adjust the realistic idea, incorporating different variables, give a refreshed rendition of their visionary graph.

Astrology for Beginners - Venus

We should take a gander at the "goddess of affection" - Venus and see what she brings when she goes into each house. Travels are additionally similar to a "climate estimate" covering everything, and everybody associated with the house who actually visits, we as a whole react unexpectedly. Keep things straightforward when a planet goes into each house.

Venus the primary: it's an ideal opportunity to ruin somehow. It's an ideal opportunity to truly consider your qualities, survey the previous year and see where your feeling of significant worth has expanded or diminished. Contingent upon which natal planets you have on the first, Look for conjunctions since Venus will urge you to work more enthusiastically or make you languid in context.

To take a model: Venus companion, your Christmas Venus, could mean the start of a sentiment! Occasions, old buddies and glad minutes are the thing to take care of appreciate them. It's an ideal opportunity to like yourself and quit agonizing over others. Dodge excess and truly consider setting up a "financial plan" for the coming year.

Venus in the second: you may wind up beginning another sentiment at this moment. You need to purchase pleasant things; you need to party, make new companions and cheerful minutes are the things to take care of now, appreciate them for you have to have a great time and make some great memories. As Venus travels through this area, they center around pay, income, costs, investment funds, values, and adoration comprehension.

Venus in the third, you will have an energy about scholarly magnificence, and it will be anything but difficult to examine your sentiments with somebody, without feeling humiliated, you may even end up telling somebody that you love them, or to chat with companions of your affection life all the more unreservedly. Your words will have a shivering of adoration or enthusiasm going through them-use it for your potential benefit. Likewise, you will start to perceive the "excellence" that encompasses you, and associations with ladies when all is said in done bring rewards that have enduring impacts.

Venus in the fourth: you will feel that others are possibly in support of you: this travel isn't enduring, to limit superfluous clash, to ten preceding going into any sort of conversation with your friends and family! Companions, family, guardians or youngsters will cause you to feel somewhat passionate (weeping for no obvious explanation). In the event that you feel eager and grouchy, go out and visit or welcome companions or places of interest.

Venus in the fifth: you would prefer not to be distant from everyone else as of now, and if your connections work out in a good way, all will be great. In the event that there are issues, they can or will emerge! You will have the ability to pull in the inverse or similar sex, so "alurve" is noticeable all around, and in the event that you are intrigued or accessible, and another adoration interest may show up not too far off - go out and mingle, make new companions and Party, Party, Party!!! Cash and new merchandise, just as new companions or sweethearts, he could be your ally. This is a decent journey for every money related action, as long as you are not lavish to utilize sound judgment and a little limitation. This should be a decent time, don't sit and trust that things will occur, go out and have a great time!

Venus in the 6th: this is a decent situation for wellbeing. If you misuse your body for egocentrism and rich and sweet nourishments, you should maintain a strategic distance from abundant sugar and starches. Sentiment and tattle about sentiment in the working environment proliferate as of now. Your contemplations become genuine during this travel, so think and act emphatically can be home for the wellbeing, recall the word embellishment in all everyday issues, and organize your day by day schedule:

mull over a best eating routine wellbeing! Hands-on front for too little discussions meddles with the work that prompts tattle, and in the event that you are searching for a raise or sitting tight for advancement, this will occur on the off chance that you are prepared and have arranged the way! Keep in mind, in the event that you beat him on the "advancement shafts" he was not prepared.

Travel to Venus in 7: you can end up beginning another sentiment right now for these special seasons; old buddies and glad minutes are the things to address. You ought to have a great time and have some good times. Try not to be excessively luxurious, gloat or be excessively eager for entertainment only and in the event that you want to purchase wonderful things think regarding needs you don't need! Mull over the buys you make for yourself and your family since it could be dull or excessively costly. Regardless of whether it's a man or a lady, there could be relationship issues with ladies or your accomplice! Think positive, be positive, and recollect, this is the House Of Attraction, and like a magnet being a magnet, you can not manage without drawing in iron.

Venus in 8: this will end up being an extraordinary period in which to dig into relationship issues or make something in a relationship that isn't generally there! Make issues in the event that you are presently seeing someone more "force" than your accomplice may have the option to give- Don't be desirous or manipulative! As this travel unfurls, you will find another you (fortunate or unfortunate, positive or negative, this is the topic of $ 60,000). You will feel lewder or, be careful with other people who are explicitly amazing! Reconsider prior to tolerating strange blessings: keep the property and monetary undertakings of con artists! Note that this is the home of revolutionary change and key with others' cash: the banks, development organizations, credit associations, or the old "uncle Frank" during this travel, do whatever it takes not to tune in to the antagonism of others.

Travel to Venus in 9: this is a decent an ideal opportunity to appreciate more music and sentiment; you ought to likewise be fortunate with cash! Numerous festivals will come to your approach to take advantage of the Times that anticipate us and appreciate the merry environment. A fortunate woman is around to search for your courtesies! Travel to unfamiliar spots, regardless of whether for a long or short remain, raise spirits, talk about such, there will be more noteworthy correspondence with the higher domains, profound domains, a revelation is likewise conceivable during this period! The future must show up and feel more splendid than it has been for quite a while.

Venus on day 10: you will feel somewhat quiet and calm during this travel, in any event, saying "farewell" to a friend or family member or, unexpectedly, meeting somebody who will end up being a companion or darling forever. On the off chance that you feel desolate or have issues with somebody you love, don't be hesitant to discuss your sentiments; any sexual restraint could cause you to feel more baffled than expected, form spans, not dividers! Reliability and discretion, particularly with more seasoned individuals from your family, will give you a great deal of internal delight. You hazard getting more traditionalist in your budgetary undertakings; this is a decent an ideal opportunity to build up a business or association that will prompt enduring achievement. On another level, you might be truly inspired by music, craftsmanship or collectibles.

The travel of Venus in the 11, sudden things occur, in old and new connections you can win or lose in all that you attempt, so take a risk, since it will make you savvier and some way or another a lot more extravagant. You will encounter peculiarities in your affection life, releasing your feelings to boundaries; there will be emotional episodes and a longing for more noteworthy autonomy! Kids or someone more youthful than you can currently drive you up the wall, so don't express the things you may lament later. Another sentiment can be noticeable all around, individuals are all the more energizing, life is additionally intriguing, and you have more opportunity to do whatever you might want to do. Be mindful so as not to turn out to be excessively fascinated or excessively energized!

Venus on the twelfth: during this travel of the twelfth you are in an illusory world, so sit tight for it to pass by to make a judgment, or to settle on genuine choices, for the occasion, attempt to appreciate anything of excellence, venture out or tune in to the little privileged insights of others. Focus on monetary or sentimental double-dealing right now since it is realized that this travel exposes the unadulterated truth to any mystery admirer. You are truly receptive now, and assuming alone or feeling a little lonely, you may be pulled into a bogus and beguiled feeling of affection, forestalled is spared! Love isn't what it appears now. Loosen up somewhat more intellectually and when negative contemplations show up in your brain, don't interface or kiss them else; you might be very nearly a mental meltdown!

You can likewise be welcome to head out to delightful spots where another dispassionate love can show up, which presents to you loads of fun and another breath throughout everyday life. Next article: accomplish astrology work for you-damages.

How To Be A Professional Astrologer

An expert stargazer has numerous deterrents while in transit to the exhibit movement of mysterious expert counsels. There are no organizations that enlist proficient soothsayers; it is an organization that will require pioneering abilities with prevalent celestial information.

Generally, you don't decide to be a crystal gazer; the calling calls you. It's actually an occupation. A future celestial prophet is compelled to share puzzles and messages from the universe to help other people with a framework that gives so much shrewdness and comprehension.

Superb preparing is fundamental to make ready for a decent stargazer. A few expert associations offer exercises that will give you admittance to the universes best and acclaimed stargazers. For Continuing Education, locate a nearby Astrology gathering or association with month to month or every other month gatherings. Numerous neighborhood prophetic gatherings will likewise have Astrology exercises for novices and intermediates. There are proficient Astrology accreditation courses offered by National Astrology associations that will quantify your degree of learning. Kepler school offers a single man and graduate degree in astrology.

In the event that you don't have a neighborhood Astrology club, pursue online courses and go to local meetings. Whenever you are acquainted with the various orders of astrology, you need to lessen your thoughtfulness regarding a visionary field that suits your disposition. You can be dependent upon mental, prescient, money related, hourly, cosmobiology, Vedic astrology, to give some examples.

Perusing is fundamental; there are many books that will help you see all the more profoundly how to decipher a chart. It is prescribed to pick creators who practice the kind of astrology that intrigues you. Whenever you've taken in your specialty, start by giving astrology letter readings to your companions to get criticism. Criticism of your abilities is basic to sharpen your insight into the book.

Being an expert stargazer is a remunerating experience; realizing that you help other people comprehend your fate and your way in life through astrology brings fulfillment. Proficient visionary discussions can help other people at various occasions of emergency and on ordinary occasions to figure out what planetary impacts are around an individual.

On the off chance that you feel the call to be an expert stargazer, show restraint toward the cycle. Getting diverse individual readings from different celestial prophets will give you a thought of the various styles of mysterious readings and help you understand what you have to do to turn into a decent stargazer. Utilize the messages on your astrology graph to help you on your approach to turning into an expert Astrology advisor.

Astrology Insights

Astrology is an incredibly old and different order and can't be managed in detail here. This rundown's motivation is to comprehend some essential ideas and eventually consolidate your craving to find out additional. There are incredible books for learners accessible that work superbly of placing astrology in wording that is effectively reasonable. Before, the majority of the books accessible were excessively specialized and hard to interpret.

Three data is required if a celestial prophet will draw an image for you: where you were conceived, your date of birth, and, if conceivable, the hour of your introduction to the world. In the event that you don't have your season of birth, the celestial prophet will at present have the option to make a graph. However, it won't be so itemized. The stargazer will draw up a table depending on the situation of the planets when you were conceived. From this picture, the individual can mention what you can expect in your life, how your adolescence was, what gifts you have, the negative parts of yourself you have survived, and your positive qualities. You can likewise, in the event that you need, what you have accomplished in this life.

In the event that you have refunds on your board, and the vast majority have at any rate one, it implies that you have not taken in certain exercises in at least one past life and have attempted once more. For instance, suppose that Mercury, the planet that oversees correspondence, is retrograde on its guide. This implies that in a past life, you confused something significant through the expressed or composed word. Perhaps you showed terrible data or composed books that were genuinely defective in the data they gave. If so, you will most likely discover in this life that you experience issues conveying. One of my customers with retrograde Mercury has dyslexia, another experiences issues conveying vocally, and another experiences issues composing.

A Christmas subject has planets, signs and houses. There are ten planets utilized in astrology, and the ten are found in every natal graph. The mysterious sign that contains each house and every planet contrasts with every individual, except these planets influence us all. The ten planets are The Sun, Moon, Mercury, Mars, Venus, Jupiter, Saturn, Neptune, Uranus and Pluto (in spite of their ongoing logical corruption!). They speak to the ten major and various manners by which we communicate, adversely or emphatically, and when this data is joined with the data spoke to by signs and houses, a definite portrayal of an individual emerges.

On the off chance that you need to find out additional, there are a huge number of approaches to do it - there are a few books, as I stated, there is the web and its abundance of data, there are workshops (I instruct actually - see the connection to one side, etc. For the most part, I recommend perusing books about the indications of the sun as a decent beginning stage. Whenever you have found out about the indications of the sun, you can continue to peruse the indications of the Moon, at that point Mercury, Mars, Venus, Jupiter, Saturn, Uranus, Neptune and Pluto. In the event that you approach slowly and carefully, you will find that astrology is a magnificent order to learn, as an item, yet in addition, as a device to assist you with getting yourself. When you do this, you can begin becoming acquainted with others around you and comprehend why they are how they are.

Why Consider Astrology Now?

Astrology is the strategy for deciding an individual's character and future through the arrangement of stars and planets. Astrology doesn't work and can't anticipate future occasions or characters. Eastern astrology is occasion arranged; they will mention to you what occurred before and what will occur later on considerably more precisely. The most boundless utilization of the astrology horoscope is to utilize it to dissect people's birth outlines to understand character, mental qualities, and, somewhat, destiny.

Astrology of the Arab time is the quick precursor of Western astrology today. Our astrology may, truth be told, be the replacement to the third current of old astrology. Created by the Greeks and dependent on a portion of the central thoughts created in Babylon, this sort of astrology is otherwise called "judge" or "genethliac". This is the type of astrology that most of us know today, in the event that we are not adherents or doubters. The topic of why individuals put stock in astrology is more intriguing than the subtleties of the horoscope. Analysts have indicated that customers are happy with celestial expectations at whatever point systems are individualized in a somewhat dubious way.

Astrology is best perceived by figuring out how it began. Astrology is, without a doubt, the most seasoned and simultaneously right now the most famous of all pseudoscience. Astrology is likewise used to extend the comprehension of our temperament. This mental methodology has expanded fundamentally in the course of recent years, as an ever-increasing number of crystal gazers build up their directing abilities. Astrology is a supernatural idea, which gave us creationism and most types of elective medication. It negates logical thinking and puts the specialist precisely contrary to the convention of edification.

Astrology is pseudoscience since individuals frequently put stock in it for ill-conceived reasons. He doesn't give models here. Astrology is, to put it plainly, the investigation of the connection between's the cosmic places of the planets and the occasions on Earth. Soothsayers accept that the places of the sun, moon and planets at the hour of the introduction of an individual affect the personality of this individual. Astrology is a brilliant mix of science, workmanship and craftsmanship. The best part about this is that regardless of the amount you learn, you will always be unable to grasp all your insight.

The confidence in astrology is that the places of certain heavenly bodies influence or relate with a character attribute of individuals. Previously, the individuals who considered astrology utilized the perception of heavenly articles and the formation of charts of their developments. No earlier information on astrology is required. The four degrees of study incorporate all the prophetic information you require from the earliest starting point to have your own effective practice. Astrology is called that since it comes from the stars; as it is called philosophy since it comes from God. To live celestially is, with a wonderful lust, to eat from the tree of information on great and evil and to carry passing to oneself.

A total list of sources of astrology is past the extent of this regularly posed inquiry, yet a few books have been incorporated. Intrigued users are welcome to visit a very loaded library. Nonetheless, since the sky was never proposed for these reasons, astrology is a hazardous and illicit practice. The exercises here are for each and every individual who needs to figure out how to do astrology and how to do Astrology. They are particularly for cynics since science necessitates that information on a subject must pass before assessment.

Since, supposing that stargazing is the investigation of the developments of divine bodies, at that point, astrology is the investigation of the impacts of these developments. Cosmologists of the antiquated world expected a division of the universe by which the higher and unchanging collections of the heavenly universes ruled the earthly or sublunar circle, where everything was mortality and change. Be that as it may, astrology is not, at this point, simply love and cash. Astrology Answers numerous different inquiries. Proficient astrology is the specialty of helping other people to enable them to discover what they are called to do.

The specialist of shamanic astrology is prepared in the unaided eye information and experience of the night sky and the consecrated rhythms, cycles, and developments of the universe. Astrology is additionally a fine art, which fits speedy representations and complex pictures of people, couples, organizations, Nations and then some. Astrology can likewise obviously have otherworldly and strict subtleties, as confirmed by investigations of antiquated Egypt. Astrology isn't logical because of the reality of precession or relocation of groups of stars. Early cosmologists didn't know about precession and consequently didn't consider it in their framework.

While it is fun, the astrology of sun oriented signs is somewhat shallow and barely helpful utilization of an intricate and antiquated science that returns a large number of years. Figure out how astrology can be utilized to educate your choices and increment your insight. Astrology is the antiquated practice and investigation of stars and planets. Its set of experiences goes back to the Babylonian time. Astrology is a model.

Complete astrology is an approach to decipher a horoscope with the goal that all viewpoints are considered. We can notice patterns in External territories, for example, proficient, money related and social necessities. That is the reason astrology is known as the "science of signs." Without a push to conquer the drive of a specific power or push of activity, the signs propose what it is probably going to be, and regardless, astrology uncovers the circumstance of patterns and certain impacts. Today, some astrology is introduced along these lines; however, this isn't accurate "conventional astrology."Did you realize that astrology was viewed as a science in the old history of man?

Astrology is anything but an idiotic old thing, strange notion or pseudo-science, however a genuine study of human experience. Its images offer a path to the impulses of human conduct, which can never be decreased to straightforward and outright equations. Maybe there is aggression since astrology stays a living practice, a genuine contender of mainstream regard and support. I trust that conventional antagonism can pass on among students of history and sociologists and that a genuine comprehension of this compelling practice and conviction. This doesn't imply that astrology is exact to anticipate human conduct or occasions to an essentially more noteworthy degree than the basic case. There are many fulfilled clients who accept that their horoscope precisely portrays them and that their crystal gazer offered them great guidance.

Astrology is innocuous; it's amusement. Whatever its previous brilliance, it currently resembles a 500 vision of the universe. Astrology is maybe the most established, and even one might say the most disregarded subject. It is the most established on the grounds that astrology was present somewhere out there; we have had the option to explore the historical backdrop of humankind. All things being equal, they like to give recounted proof stories that individuals tell about how precise they think astrology is. The episodic proof isn't satisfactory in genuine science since it is too simple even to consider omitting all the pessimistic encounters that individuals have, and individuals are not awesome at precisely recalling and revealing encounters.

Astrology depends on birth cards for a person. The sun, moon, and planets are followed in the Zodiac at the hour of birth. Additionally, astrology is certainly not a fast report. Conservatives used to state that it takes an understudy a travel Saturn, around 30 years of age, to turn into a specialist. Vedic astrology is essential for an all-encompassing and coordinated information framework, and its belongings can be upgraded by collaborating with its "sister" sciences. The Vedic astrology framework is caring in light of the fact that not exclusively makes an individual mention to you what could occur, yet they are given elite of potential cures or restorative measures to make up for the sum and nature of karma returning to them, as found in the natal outline.

Astrology and the Renaissance

To lay it out plainly, one would be enticed to state that this article on astrology in the Renaissance starts with Petrarch (1304-1374) and closes with Shakespeare (1564-1616). Petrarch, "the main man of the Renaissance," was not a devotee of astrology and restricted to his fatalistic tendencies. "Free the methods of truth and life... these fireballs can't be guides for us... Enlightened by these beams, we needn't bother with these tricky soothsayers and lying prophets who void the coffers of guileless pupils of Gold, who stun their ears with jabber, attempt to degenerate with their mix-ups, stop our current life, and distress individuals with bogus feelings of trepidation of the future. It is imperative to note from the earliest starting point that the progressions made in the Renaissance had a horde of appearances. As Richard Tarnas pushed in the enthusiasm of the soul of the West, " the marvel of resurrection lies in the extraordinary variety of its looks and in its remarkable quality. However, the Renaissance isn't communicated uniquely through writing (or simultaneously or spot of the occasion) through workmanship, philosophy, the thriving of Science and disclosure.

Pondering the Renaissance and its wonders in craftsmanship, music and writing and astrology, it is critical to shoulder as a main priority that the prominent changes of that time happened with regards to torment, war, strict battles, financial downturn, the Inquisition, and religious connivances. In this huge field, in this intriguing time of history, we will attempt to decide the restored interest and advancement of astrology during the Renaissance.

Twin Stars: a change from Aristotle to Plato

The disclosure and interpretation of old writings was an agitator of incredible changes ever, especially crafted by Plato and Aristotle. In his book, sleepwalkers, Arthur Koestler remarked on the impact and prevalence of these Greek scholars. "Concerning their impact later on," composes

Koestler, " Plato and Aristotle should be called Twin Stars with a solitary focus of gravity, which encompass and substitute anticipating their light upon the ages that follow them. Each would have their chance to appreciate being "trendy" while the other is outdated. As per Koestler, Plato would rule sovereign until the twelfth century;at that point, Aristotle's work would be rediscovered and following two centuries when the world's masterminds burnt out on Aristotle's manner of speaking, Plato would return in an alternate perspective. In the period up to the ascent of the Renaissance, he was Aristotle's star to sparkle and, in spite of the fact that it could be difficult to accept, given the absence of endorsement of present-day Christianity, to astrology, he was a school scholar, who joined Aristotle, church regulation and astrology.

Thomas Aquinas (1225-1274) appeared to have been in the perfect spot at the perfect time with the correct comments. Arabic education and the conceivable interpretation of Aristotle's work into middle age Latin implied a resurrection for the Aristotelian idea during Aquinas' lifetime. These works of Aristotle turned into a significant task for this Dominican priest, a student of Albert Magnus (1206-1280), himself an Aristotelian interpreter. Tarnas noticed that Aquinas changed Aristotle over to Christianity and immersed him. The rise of the Aristotelian idea in bygone eras profited astrology in light of its view that all that occurs in the sublunar world is caused and represented by the developments of the heavenly circles. Brahe's disclosures negated the idea of a different "sublunar world". Mama, there was as yet the arrangement of divine bodies on Earth and, subsequently, they affect life on Earth. Astrology and speculative chemistry utilized these equivalent techniques for an Aristotelian rationale; however were not limited by the precision of the scholarly or totally subject to the creed of the Church: old-style Astrology, regularly connected to clinical examinations and arranged by Ptolemy, was instructed in colleges.

Unquestionably, you may have figured; your persuasions would have been more noteworthy.

Aquinas was certain and clear about the impacts of the stars as they were seen at that point: "most men... they are represented by their interests, which rely upon substantial hunger; in them, the impact of the stars is unmistakably felt. Not many shrewd men can oppose their impulses animals. Es to state, there was an immediate relationship between's what occurred in paradise and what occurred on Earth. Aquino added the significant and paramount words:

Celestial prophets, subsequently, can anticipate reality as a rule, particularly when they make general expectations. Specifically, expectations don't arrive at sureness since nothing keeps a man from opposing the diktats of his lower resources. In this manner, celestial prophets themselves regularly state that "the sages rule the stars" since, that is, the way they rule their own interests."

This stays away from the quandary that would trouble humanists in the following century: choice.

Indeed, even with Aquinas' help, this doesn't imply that the congregation upheld all aspects of astrology: there were very clear limits. While asking too profoundly, clinical astrology was satisfactory, later on, maybe viewed as strolling on God's fingers when Aquinas had painstakingly accommodated Astrology/Astronomy and the congregation giving the state of choice instead of supreme determinism.

At the beginning of the Renaissance, there is no uncertainty that astrology reemerged in spite of being ridiculed all the while in three totally different societies. Notwithstanding Petrarch's remarks, the Muslim researcher Ibn Khaldun (1332-1406) denounced astrology as "all guesses and guesses dependent on astral impact (expected to exist) and the subsequent cooling. The Frenchman Nicholas Oresme, in 1370, composed " numerous sovereigns and magnates, moved by a harmful interest, attempt with vain expressions to look for concealed things and examine what's to come. For these men (counting Petrarch), astrology has put the staggering allurement before man to find his future. Having set up the presence of astrology before the Renaissance, the subject of how it picked up prevalence regardless of being so profoundly denounced remains.

One clue lies in a connection made between heaven and Earth in a more metaphorical sense. Aquinas had pointed out that there was a " principle of continuity "(as it will be called later) that connected higher beings with life forms increasingly lower than the kingdoms of Lucifer, elements of the orthodox doctrines of the Catholic Church. This was associated with a shift from another worldly asceticism to a positive view of life and, therefore, worthy of study. We can see this new vision reflected in Dante's Divine Commedia (1265-1321), with man at the center of an Aristotelian universe, balanced between heaven and Hell in a moral drama of Christianity.

It should be noted that the universe of Aristotle, as well as that of Dante and Aquinas, was geocentric, a premise that, of course, would eventually be refuted. Dante's popular work shows how the "common" man of the time considered astronomy and theology to be inextricably linked, and, in a clear break in clerical tradition, it was written in a vernacular that even the most illiterate of the time could appreciate. Therefore, what was once only available to the higher classes or clergy had been made available to the general public.

Tarnas pointed out that if Dante's work culminated and summed up the medieval era, Petrarch " expected and propelled a future era, bringing a revival of Culture, Creativity and human greatness. According to Tarnas, Petrarch was motivated by a new spirit but inspired by the ancients to create even greater glory with man himself as the center of God's creation. Petrarch's ideal was erudite piety and called to memory the classical heritage of Europe through literature.

Even when the plague broke out, the idea that life should be appreciated rather than simply studied was evident in the work of Giovanni Boccaccio in The Decameron (1353). Boccace wrote about what life really was, rather than how the church thought it should be lived. The uncertainty of daily survival has created a general mood of morbidity, influencing people to "live for the moment."It would seem that even Petrarch was not immune to this new way of seeing life. In 1336, Petrarch climbed Mount Ventoux, which rises to more than six thousand feet, beyond the Vaucluse for the greatest pleasure of it. He read The Confessions of St. Augustine at the summit and reflected that his ascension was nothing more than an allegory of the aspiration for a better life. In his experience, perhaps we can understand why he was reluctant to accept being limited by destiny and refuse to see himself "if it has no consequences in relation to God, the church or nature."

During the years of the plague, when Europe turned its eyes to the authority of Medicine at that time, the members of the College of Physicians of Paris delivered (in part) this reason for the Great Plague:

"From the astral influence that was considered the origin of the "great mortality" doctors and scientists were as fully convinced as they were of its reality. A great conjunction of the three higher planets, Saturn, Jupiter and Mars, in the sign of Aquarius, which took place, according to Guy de Chauliac, on March 24, 1345, was generally received as its main cause."

Petrarch was disappointed to realize that the plague he had claimed from so many people he loved was caused by large conjunction of planets in the air signals.

By the fifteenth century, Astrology had received an additional boost in the form of a Byzantine scholarship. In 1438, the Byzantine Emperor John VIII Palaeologus attended the Council of Ferrara and the Council of Florence to discuss a union of the Greek and Roman churches. With him was

Plato's erudite, plethon who generously offered to translate Plato's texts to interested Florentines. It was a fabulous improvement to the previous work on the translation of Petrarch and his contemporaries, as they were so hampered by their difficulties in translating Greek into Latin. Plethon (also known as George Gemistos) had "long nurtured an ambitious plan to restore the vitality of the pagan religion that belonged before Justinian's suppression of worship and the Athens Academy: in short, he was, in everything but the name, a "pagan" philosopher. As a total pagan, Plethon predicted that the world would forget Jesus and

Cosimo de mici, head of the influential family bank Medici (who built his business empire in the economic depression after the bubonic plague) was so impressed by this "new" met opened an Academy platonic in 1439, and elected the promising young Marsilio Ficino (1433-1499) to manage it. Although, as a child, Ficino showed an early talent for translation and was encouraged by the Medici family, he eventually translated a large number of ancient texts, including those of Plato and Hermes Trismegistus. Campion points out that Greek manuscripts also found their way west after the fall of Constantinople to the Turks in 1453. Because he had established himself as an interpreter, Many of these texts fell directly into Ficino's hands.

Ficino not only interpreted these texts but commented and was clearly influenced by them. His own contributions include three books on life ("De Triplici Vita"), which contains a book entitled on obtaining life from heaven ("De Vita Coelitus Comparanda"). Ficino was largely responsible for bringing back the Neoplatonic belief that the stars were divine. Reflections of this belief can be seen in the works of Michelangelo (1475-1564), Raphael (1483-1520), DaVinci (1452-1519), Botticelli (1445-1510) and others. There was a general change in art during this period: previous artists had focused on recreating biblical images or symbols, while Renaissance artists began to study more closely the pattern of nature and to employ more realism in their work adding more color and depth as Baigent so eloquently expressed Ficino's influence on these painters, a talisman capable of changing those who contemplated it. Frances Yates thus describes Botticelli's work and, in particular, his masterpiece, The Birth Of Venus, as a practical application of Ficino's magic by drawing " the venereal spirit of the star and transmitting it to the user or the viewer of its beautiful image.

Under this resurgence of neo-Platonism and a revival of pagan gods and goddesses, Astrology had also found favor through the use of almanacs and their popularity in various European courts. Without almanacs, astrology could have continued to be available only to those who could afford to read and write (i.e., royalty) had there not been one thing: The Invention of Johann Gutenberg's printing press in 1440. Until then, the printed material, limited to the religious material copied on parchment, whose creation was taken as an act of worship (The Book Of Kells, for example), was reproduced by hand and, therefore, quite rare. For example, an inventory of books from the University of Cambridge library 1424 showed that the University owned only 122 books, each of which had a value equal to a farm or vineyard. The printing press allowed the reproduction of religious and secular texts. Astrological tables and almanacs were just one facet of the many themes that were suddenly made available to the new avid readers.

The tip of the attack

Along these lines, astrology, with its inferences to agnostic divine beings and goddesses, arrived at the pinnacle of its notoriety. Similarly, as one would have suspected astrology would be sheltered, an extraordinary after death assault came in 1494, conveyed by a Ficino understudy, Pico Della Mirandola. The pinnacle assault that has shaken astrology to the heart is as yet referred to as the most decimating assault of astrology ever. Cornelius described spike's assault as a "neo-Platonic understanding of enchantment, utilizing the weapons of Aristotelian rationale," adding that right now in our set of experiences, the innovative cognizance called wizardry and the art of horoscopic decisions were isolated... After the pinnacle, Horoscope creates never had a genuine scholarly case.

There are some regular misguided judgments about this assault. This was positively terrible information for astrology in Italy. Be that as it may, for instance, in England, in the following century, Elizabeth I straightforwardly counseled the performer John Dee (1527-1608) for celestial exhortation. During Dee's stay in France, Jean-Baptiste Morin (1583-1659) delighted in, as Dee, countless supporters in Europe. Also, the assault was not coordinated against astrology itself, yet against the maltreatment of handy stargazers. Campion calls attention to that Pico's expectation was more to change astrology than to wreck it. This prophetic turn of events, similar to some other Reformation, will at last zero in on numerous celestial practices, for example, mistaken cosmic tables and a geocentric universe, just as improvements outside the Ptolemaic framework, for example, new house frameworks.

It can not be prevented that the standing from getting astrology had an incredible accomplishment with Johann Stoeffler's forecast of an extraordinary flood during the extraordinary combination of the planets with Pisces in February 1524, a month known for its fine climate. In spite of the fact that the late spring saw some prominent downpours, it was a long way from the extraordinary flood expectations that in excess of fifty soothsayers had anticipated after Stoeffler's forecasts. In any case, this did little to kill the standing of Nostradamus (1503-1566), whose groups of four were notable in his life.

The progressive thought of Nicolas Copernicus (1473-1543) of a universe fixated on The Sun established little connection when, in the insurgencies of the heavenly circles, it was distributed in 1543. Koestler says that Copernicus was a difficult task to peruse in addition to the fact that He was an awful merchant. Notwithstanding, in the long run, this work would change man's perspective on the world from a Kosmos (in the Greek sense), where there was a proportionality among man and the universe, to the post-Renaissance heliocentric World related with the advancement of current science. Astrology requires this scale among man and the universe to flourish. With Galileo's blockbuster in 1609,

Siderius Nuncius, the heliocentric perspective was slung into public cognizance.

Around 31 years after Copernicus ' passing on November 11, 1572, Tycho Brahe, leaving a catalytic research facility to get his supper, saw another splendid star close to the heavenly body Cassiopeus. About this occasion, says Koestler:

"The importance of the thrilling occasion was in the way that it negated the fundamental tenet, Aristotelian, dispassionate and Christian-that all change, all age and rot were limited in the quick region of the earth, the circle sub-lunar; where, as the eighth far off circle wherein were put the fixed stars was permanent from the day of creation."

Brahe's examination had one element hard to track down in Aristotelian rationale: accuracy. The rationale of time underscores quality instead of quantitative estimation; Brahe gives himself to estimation, down to portions of Arc minutes in his computations, and doesn't endure the "sufficiently nearby" demeanor of planetary tables. Afterward,

Brahe demonstrated that the Great Comet of 1577 was not a sub-lunar article (the Aristotelian idea of time) yet was "at any rate multiple times" in space as much as the moon. In the very year, Brahe, at his solicitation, gotten the main watch with a brief hand from his innovator, Jost Burgi. As yet ever, the exact upkeep of time had been inconceivable.

A couple of years after the fact, Astrology actually experienced the Papal Bull of 1585, which, truth be told, precluded legal astrology and directed the conclusion of all genuine mysterious distributions aside from the least difficult of handouts (very similar things Pico questioned). As a genuinely customary, if not traditionalist, discipline, astrology has not been helped by a significant change in outlook in cosmology. At the point when a cold and hungry Johannes Kepler (1571-1630) showed up at the door of Brahe in 1600, it was inevitable that the world was persuaded that the earth spun around the sun.

On the off chance that the "logical" side of astrology started to disentangle, it barely impacted the love of the Elizabethan crowd for this. William Shakespeare makes in excess of a hundred suggestions to astrology in his 37 plays. Now is the ideal time; planets and stars were represented, glorious circles had everlasting spirits, and individuals were hesitant to change the conventional Order of things. "The sky themselves, the planets and this middle notice degree need and spot... be that as it may, when the planets in terrible combinations of turmoil meander, what bothers and what presence!" Another case of this can be found in the tempest of Shakespeare; for example, The performer of the achievement (a character approximately dependent on the celestial prophet of Queen Elizabeth, John Dee), is depicted as the reason for an extraordinary tempest and ensuing sinking, with the incredible consternation of his young little girl, Miranda. It appears to be such an unexpected, however kind, accolade for astrology that the characters of this work were utilized to name the satellites of the planet Uranus when they were found in the XIX century. It could nearly resemble an olive branch, from cosmology to astrology.

Helpful Advice On How To Learn Astrology

The ideal approach to learn astrology is to contemplate the current celestial areas of planets and comprehend the connection between emblematic portrayals of planetary models and political, natural and get-togethers planets.

Astrology tip number one: follow recent developments.

By following current prophetic developments and changes, you will get a thought of the various places of the planets and comprehend the various manners by which these arrangements show themselves. For instance, today, there is an incredible setup that speaks to progressive and sickening thoughts; at the point when the planets adjusted and moved to these positions, the dissent in the Middle East. At the point when you study astrology by following the current places of the planets, you won't simply have the option to foresee or comprehend world occasions, yet you will likewise have the option to decipher how these planetary models play on close to home visionary guides.

Astrology tip number two. Comprehend and track travels to your astrology card.

Notwithstanding following the planets' current celestial developments, it is imperative to follow the prophetic energies corresponding to your own outline. When a planet in a current situation in the sky makes a numerical corner for a planet's Natal situation on the astrology diagram, then your own planet is under an astrology travel. For instance, on the off chance that you were brought into the world with your Sun in Aries and Uranus in Aries is in a similar degree as your Sun, at that point, you are under the travel of Uranus to your Sun. Particularly Uranus joins your Sun. This would demonstrate a second in your life for your own "insurgency" of progress.

Astrology Tip Number Three: locate a decent Astrology course or astrology workshop.

There are numerous approaches to contemplate astrology, yet it tends to be extremely perplexing and befuddling on the off chance that you don't have a framework that permits you to learn Astrology effectively and easily. Despite the fact that likewise, with any new encouragement, gaining information requires a little exertion; however, the ideal path is to gain from an accomplished stargazer who makes confounded ideas justifiable. Discover an astrology course that is planned around astrology's current standards and how mysterious impacts influence the astrology graph. Discover a soothsayer you love and an astrology educator who has insight. Obviously, you can gain from somebody you don't care for; however, why? It is better not to have a character boundary between you and the subject you are learning.

Astrology tip number four:

Compose your biography. Likely the most ideal approach to learn astrology is to make a personal history of the occasions that happened in your life.

Take as much time as necessary to truly recollect significant minutes and all the recollections you can. Like the first occasion when you became hopelessly enamored, graduation, your first work, any significant employment changes, getting hitched, having kids, getting separated, enormous or sad romantic tales, moving, voyaging. Enter the dates of these occasions. So you will do a review Astrology task to figure out what travels or planetary impacts were happening around then.

Astrology Council number five: go to astrology meetings.

There is nothing similar to going to astrology meetings to experience the intricacy and variety that astrology offers. Search for territorial and public gatherings offered around the nation, or in the event that you have a solid Jupiter, Research Astrology meetings around the globe, why not? It is amusing to contemplate astrology with similar stargazers who meet at Astrology meetings. Notwithstanding astrology exercises, numerous meetings offer astrology workshops when the gathering.

Astrology is a captivating teach and can be overpowering when you begin learning Astrology. Try not to let intricacy disappoint you by learning this lovely endowment of the universe that can help you get yourself and your general surroundings. Figure out how to be a co-maker with the ground-breaking powers of the planets. Learn Astrology, be your celestial prophet and expert this mystery and old control of obscure information and instinct.

Vedic Astrology Helps Steer Key Life Decisions

We as a whole have worries about our future, life, family, abundance and wellbeing. A large number of us react to our own and expert concerns utilizing the impact of astrology. While astrology is a genuinely broad field with numerous branches and religions, Vedic astrology is viewed as a solid conviction framework that started in India hundreds of years back. Today, Vedic astrology comprises a significant conviction framework and strategy for direction for some individuals, both in India and in nations, for example, the United States, United Kingdom, Canada, Australia, and so on

When all is said in done, it is accepted that the majority of the mishaps; misfortunes, misfortunes, ailments and deferrals are brought about via planetary developments or "yoga" which are in ominous positions. Diverse planetary positions cause mysterious circumstances, to be specific, KaalSarp Dosh, Manglik Dosh, Pitra Dosh, Sade Sati. It is said that a large number of these mysterious positions are liable for causing changes in marriage, life, sentiment, vocations and instruction. Since astrology isn't a precise science and information on specific mysterious understandings isn't normal, there have been situations when the realities have been confounded. Exact understanding and mediation in Vedic astrology require exceptional experience and practice.

Vedic astrology as a control tends to all parts of human life: otherworldly, physical, mental and enthusiastic. The premise of Vedic astrology depends on planetary developments and positions regarding time and its effect on living creatures on Earth. In Vedic astrology, there are 27 groups of stars, including the 12 indications of the zodiac, 9 planets and 12 houses, each house and Planet represents one part of human life, and an individual, time, spot of birth demonstrates how the 12 signs are appropriated between the 12 houses and 9 planets. The guide, which speaks to signs and planets, is generally known as a horoscope graph.

For quite a long time, Vedic astrology has been utilized as an extraordinary forecast and estimations arrangement. These estimations depend on the places of stars and planets and are in stage for every zodiac sign under which people can be conceived. Vedic astrology permits individuals to distinguish what could occur in their future carries on with and encourages potential solutions to help the circumstance. The thought behind the conviction is to distinguish approaching dangers and stay away from them before they happen. The Hindu celestial prophet utilizes proper and exact devices to distinguish pieces of information in a person's life that could help them stay away from specific mishaps that happen. Celestial prophets frequently use birth cards to anticipate the Bhavishya (fate) of an element. The Vedic soothsayer says that Indian Vedic astrology additionally follows the Dasha framework, which depends on the Native Moon in the natal outline. It is additionally viewed as an exact pointer of future occasions.

Understanding the connection between planets, stars and chakras, celestial prophets see where energy streams or matter doesn't stream. This can be identified with all types of mending, regardless of whether passionate, sexual, physical, karmic, mental or lively. In these innovatively progressed times, we can discover numerous assets and instruments to decide our Bhavishya. The Internet has allowed us the chance to contact live soothsayers and find what lies on our route, all from the solace of our home. Vedic astrology can assist us with seeing our actual guidelines of soul level throughout everyday life.

Printed in Great Britain
by Amazon